# Soutach

## Creating Art with Thread and Beads

**Mary R. Mackenzie**

# Introduction

## The Allure of Soutache Jewelry

Soutache jewelry is a celebration of elegance, precision, and artistry. Rooted in centuries-old tradition, soutache began as a decorative braid used to embellish military uniforms and garments. Over time, it found a new home in the world of high fashion and jewelry, where it transformed into a medium for intricate, eye-catching designs that reflect a blend of classic sophistication and modern flair. Today, soutache jewelry appeals to crafters and fashion enthusiasts alike for its unique combination of vibrant color, intricate detail, and versatile style.

At its core, soutache is a technique that involves layering and stitching together flat, corded braids typically crafted from rayon, silk, or cotton around a central focal piece, such as a bead or cabochon. These cords, or "soutache," give jewelry a distinct, flowing design that brings elegance and movement to each piece. With its graceful lines and vibrant colors, soutache jewelry is beloved for its ability to add a touch of luxury and personality to any outfit.

For beginners, soutache jewelry is accessible and endlessly rewarding. Unlike other forms of jewelry making that require metalworking or advanced tools, creating soutache pieces mainly relies on basic tools and a willingness to explore new techniques. Starting with simple shapes and basic stitches, beginners can create wearable art that looks as intricate as it is beautiful, even with minimal experience.

In this book, we'll embark on a journey to explore the art of soutache jewelry-making from the very basics to more complex designs. Each chapter is designed to guide you step-by-step, so you can develop confidence in the craft while creating beautiful pieces. From the first stitch to your final, polished piece, you'll gain the skills needed to bring your own unique visions to life and make jewelry that's as elegant as it is personal. Whether you're crafting for yourself, for friends, or to start your own collection, this guide will help you master the fundamentals and fall in love with the timeless art of soutache jewelry.

Let's get started and dive into the enchanting world of soutache!

# Chapter One

## Getting to Know Soutache

In this chapter, we'll cover the essentials you need to start creating stunning soutache jewelry. From understanding the origins and purpose of soutache to selecting materials and tools, this chapter lays the groundwork for your journey into the art of soutache jewelry.

**What is Soutache?**

- **Origins and History**
  Soutache, also known as "Russian braid" or "gimp," is a decorative cord that has its roots in Eastern European and Middle Eastern garment design. Originally used as a trimming on military uniforms and

formal attire, it served both functional and decorative purposes. Over the centuries, soutache evolved beyond clothing into fine art and, eventually, jewelry, gaining popularity in high fashion for its delicate yet striking appearance.

- **Soutache in Jewelry**
  In jewelry-making, soutache is used as both a decorative element and a structural component, creating intricate, flowing designs around beads, cabochons, and other focal pieces. Its flexibility allows for endless creative possibilities, from simple loops and shapes to complex layered patterns. Understanding the origins of soutache adds depth to the craft, as each piece you make

carries forward a rich tradition in a modern, wearable form.

## Materials

- **Soutache Cords**

  Soutache cords are the foundation of soutache jewelry. They come in a variety of materials most commonly rayon, cotton, and silk. Rayon is popular for its smooth texture and slight sheen, which add elegance to jewelry designs. Cotton soutache has a matte finish and is ideal for a more subtle look, while silk cords offer a luxurious feel and a rich color palette. When choosing cords, consider thickness, color, and flexibility, as these factors affect the look and feel of your final piece.

- **Beads, Crystals, and Cabochons**
  Adding beads and other decorative elements gives soutache jewelry its signature style. From sparkling crystals to gemstone cabochons, selecting the right focal pieces can elevate your design and bring a piece to life. Look for items that match your chosen color palette and overall design theme, as well as those that are easy to secure within your cords. For beginners, start with medium-sized beads and flat-back cabochons that can be easily anchored within your design.
- **Thread and Other Essentials**
  The type of thread you choose is crucial, as it holds your piece together and provides durability. Nylon and polyester threads are

popular choices for their strength, while cotton and silk threads work well for lightweight pieces. In addition to thread, you'll need glue, usually a fast-drying fabric or jewelry adhesive, to help secure knots and edges.

## Tools of the Trade

1. **Basic Tools**

   Getting started with soutache jewelry requires only a few simple tools:

- **Beading Needles**: Fine, flexible needles make it easier to work through tight spaces and ensure precision.
- **Scissors**: Sharp scissors specifically for fabric and thread provide clean cuts.

- **Glue**: Jewelry glue or fabric adhesive is helpful for reinforcing and securing knots or finishing pieces.

2. **Optional Tools**

   These tools can make the process smoother and improve the quality of your work:

- **Tweezers**: Handy for handling small beads and cords, especially in more intricate designs.

- **Magnifying Glass or Light**: Useful if you're working on detailed designs, as they help reduce eye strain.

- **Bead Mat or Board**: A work surface that keeps beads and cords from rolling away, helping with organization and design planning.

## Types of Soutache Jewelry

- **Common Styles and Pieces**
  Soutache jewelry can take many forms, from earrings and pendants to bracelets and brooches. Beginners often start with small pieces like earrings and pendants to learn basic techniques before moving on to larger projects.
- **Understanding the Components of a Soutache Piece**
  Each soutache piece generally consists of a focal element (like a cabochon or large bead), a frame created by stitching soutache cords, and decorative accents or smaller beads. Once you understand the elements involved, creating designs becomes much easier, as you can plan and adjust based on these core components.

# Choosing Your First Project

- **Planning for Success**

  For your first project, choose a simple design with just a few cords and beads. Focusing on smaller pieces, like earrings or a single pendant, allows you to get comfortable with the basic techniques without feeling overwhelmed.

- **Color, Texture, and Design Considerations**

  Selecting colors and textures is one of the most exciting parts of the design process. Start with two or three complementary colors to create a balanced look. For your first project, avoid overly intricate designs; instead, focus on learning how to work with the cords, control the tension, and create smooth, even loops.

# Chapter Two

## Essential Techniques and Stitches

This chapter will walk you through the core techniques and stitches essential to creating beautiful soutache jewelry. From setting up your cords to mastering foundational stitches and shaping methods, these techniques will equip you with the skills needed to bring your designs to life.

**Setting Up for Success**

- **Preparing Your Cords**

  before you start stitching, it's crucial to prepare your soutache cords. Trim them to a workable length typically between 10 to 20 inches, depending on your design. To prevent fraying, use a fabric glue or lighter to seal the ends carefully. Align the cords side by side, ensuring they're flat and even, as this alignment will give your design a clean, professional look.

- **Choosing and Threading Your Needle**

  Select a fine, flexible beading needle that can easily pass through the cords and beads without creating tension. Use a strong nylon or polyester thread in a color that matches your cords to create a seamless look, threading your needle with an arm's length of thread to avoid tangling.

## Basic Stitches for Beginners

- **Straight Stitch**

  The straight stitch is the foundation

of soutache jewelry. This stitch attaches cords to each other and secures beads within the design. To start, align two or more cords side by side, and bring the needle up from the back to the front, sewing through the center channel of each cord. Continue stitching along the length of the cord, keeping stitches small and even for a consistent, professional look.

- **Backstitch**

The backstitch helps reinforce connections between cords and provides extra stability, especially around focal beads. To make a backstitch, insert your needle back through the previous stitch, bringing it forward to continue stitching along the cords. This technique also allows you to make slight adjustments to the shape of the cords, which is useful for creating curves and circles.

- **Edge Beading**
Edge beading is used to add decorative beads along the outer edge of your cords, framing the design and giving it a polished appearance. Thread a small bead onto your needle, stitch through the edge of the cord to secure it, and repeat along the entire length. This technique can add texture and color to your piece and help define its outline.

## Working with Beads

- **Attaching Focal Beads**
Focal beads, like cabochons or

crystals, are typically placed in the center of the design. To attach a focal bead, position it between your cords and secure it with a few straight stitches. For a neat finish, sew the cords around the bead's edge, framing it securely.

- **Adding Spacer Beads**

  Spacer beads are small beads used to add detail and space out other elements. To add spacer beads, stitch them directly between layers of cords, spacing them evenly to maintain balance in the design. This technique can be used to highlight certain areas or add a touch of sparkle and dimension.

## Shaping and Layering

- **Building Curves and Loops**

  One of the defining features of soutache jewelry is its flowing, curved shapes. To create curves, gently bend the cords as you stitch, keeping your tension consistent to avoid puckering. Practice small loops and tighter curves before working on more complex shapes.

- **Layering Techniques**

  Layering cords adds depth and interest to your designs. Start by stitching a row of cords around a focal bead, then add additional layers of cords around the initial row, securing each layer with small, even stitches. Adjust the number of layers based on the desired complexity and thickness of your design.

- **Securing Loose Ends**

  As you complete each section, secure loose ends with a small drop of glue and a tight knot. Tuck the ends between layers to conceal them, and then trim any excess carefully for a clean finish.

## Tips for Clean and Consistent Stitching

- **Controlling Tension**

  Consistent tension is key to achieving a professional look in soutache jewelry. Avoid pulling stitches too tightly, which can cause puckering, and don't leave them too loose, as this may weaken the piece.

Practice stitching with even, gentle tension to develop control.

- **Aligning Cords**

  To maintain the symmetry of your design, keep your cords aligned side by side as you stitch. Regularly check your work from the front to ensure each layer stays aligned, making small adjustments as needed to keep the cords flat.

- **Finishing and Securing**

  When you complete a section or finish a project, tie off the thread securely and add a small dot of glue to secure the final knot. Conceal any visible thread or loose ends within the layers of cords for a seamless appearance.

## Practice Exercise: Making a Basic Design Element

- **Goal**: Create a simple spiral design with a small focal bead.
- **Materials Needed**: Two colors of soutache cord, one small bead, needle, matching thread, and scissors.
- **Steps**:
1. Begin by threading your needle and preparing two pieces of cord, each about 12 inches long.
2. Position the focal bead between the cords, securing it with a few straight stitches.
3. Begin wrapping the cords around the bead in a spiral, stitching between the cords every few millimeters to keep them tight against the bead.

4. Continue wrapping until you reach the desired size, then secure and trim the ends.
5. Inspect your work, making small adjustments to ensure symmetry and smoothness.

**Practice Exercise: Creating an Edge Beaded Accent**

- **Goal**: Practice adding decorative beads along the edge of a cord layer.
- **Materials Needed**: Soutache cord, small decorative beads, needle, matching thread, and scissors.
- **Steps**:
1. Begin by stitching a row of soutache cord to form the outer edge of your design.

2. Thread a small bead, stitch it onto the edge, and repeat at regular intervals along the cord.
3. Continue beading the entire length of the cord, adjusting spacing as needed.
4. Secure and trim any excess thread, then inspect the edge for consistency.

# Chapter Three

## Getting Creative with Color and Design

In this chapter, you'll learn to harness the power of color, texture, and creative planning to bring originality to your soutache jewelry. From understanding color theory basics to experimenting with design ideas, you'll discover how to make pieces that are uniquely yours. We'll also explore tips for incorporating beads and other embellishments that complement your chosen palette and style.

**Choosing Color Schemes**

1. **Understanding Color Theory Basics**

   Knowing a bit about color theory will help you create harmonious and visually appealing designs. Start by familiarizing yourself with the color wheel, which includes:

- **Complementary Colors**: Opposite colors on the wheel (like blue and orange) that create vibrant contrast.

- **Analogous Colors**: Colors next to each other on the wheel (such as blue and green) that provide a subtle, harmonious blend.

- **Monochromatic Colors**: Variations of a single color, from light to dark, which can lend a sophisticated look to a piece. When selecting colors, think about the mood you want to convey bold colors create high energy, while softer hues suggest elegance.

2. **Selecting Cords and Beads in Cohesive Colors**

Choose soutache cords, beads, and focal pieces that work well together within your selected color scheme. To keep the design cohesive, limit your palette to two or three colors. Adding metallic accents like gold, silver, or copper can add sophistication and tie different colors together.

3. **Creating Depth with Tones and Shades**

Incorporating different shades and tones of your chosen colors can add depth and interest to your piece. For example, pairing a light, medium, and dark shade of blue will give a monochromatic design added dimension. This technique can be especially effective in layered designs where each color builds on the last.

**Designing Your First Piece**

- **Sketching Your Idea**

  Begin by sketching your design on paper, focusing on basic shapes, patterns, and the arrangement of focal beads. This is especially useful for beginners as it provides a clear plan to follow. Start with simple shapes like spirals, loops, and borders around a central bead or cabochon, which are both easy to execute and visually appealing.

- **Balancing Symmetry and Asymmetry**

  Decide if you'd like a symmetrical or asymmetrical design. Symmetrical designs offer balance and can be easier to execute as you mirror each side, while asymmetrical designs allow more creative freedom and can add a modern twist. Regardless of the approach, aim to balance the piece by evenly distributing color and texture.

- **Working with Layers and Levels**
Layering cords and beads in a gradual manner adds structure and richness to your design. Plan each layer to either emphasize the focal point or create an intricate frame around it. Sketching out where each layer will go in advance can prevent overcrowding and help you achieve a balanced look.

## Incorporating Beads and Embellishments

- **Choosing the Right Beads**

  Beads are the centerpiece of many soutache designs, so select beads that not only complement your color scheme but also vary in size and texture. Round, faceted, and cabochon-style beads are excellent for adding different effects, with faceted beads providing sparkle, while flat-back cabochons offer a smooth, elegant finish.

- **Adding Texture with Decorative Elements**

  Don't hesitate to mix in various bead types like pearls, crystals, or seed beads to add dimension and texture. By choosing elements that vary in shine and opacity, you can make your piece more engaging and visually complex. Adding sequins or metallic findings can introduce an extra layer of embellishment for a more ornate look.

- **Positioning Beads for Maximum Effect**

  To create a balanced design, place larger beads near the center or focal points, and use smaller beads to highlight edges or as accent details. Experiment by arranging beads on your sketch before stitching, giving you a preview of the finished look. Use spacing strategically to keep the design from feeling overcrowded, allowing the beauty of each element to shine.

# Creating Movement and Flow

- **Emphasizing Natural Shapes**

  One of the unique aspects of soutache is its fluidity. Use this flexibility to create natural shapes like waves, spirals, or curves that give your piece a sense of movement. These shapes can guide the eye and make the design feel more organic.

- **Building Layers of Cords in a Flowing Pattern**

  To create a piece that feels cohesive and dynamic, layer your cords in a pattern that follows the curves of the focal bead or main design element. Layered curves and repeated patterns naturally draw the eye, adding both flow and visual impact.

- **Using Loops and Swirls to Guide the Eye**

  Incorporating loops and swirls into your design creates a sense of direction and energy. For example, loops framing a focal bead can emphasize the center, while swirls along the edge guide the viewer's gaze around the piece. Practice creating balanced swirls that add flair without overwhelming the design.

**Practice Exercise: Planning a Colorful Earring Design**

- **Goal**: Sketch and plan a simple earring design with a central bead and complementary colors.
- **Materials Needed**: Colored pencils or markers, paper, and a ruler.

- **Steps**:
1. Begin by sketching the central bead and decide on a color scheme.
2. Plan layers of soutache cords around the bead, sketching each layer in a different color.
3. Add small circles along the cords to represent accent beads, experimenting with placements until balanced.
4. Visualize the design with colored pencils or markers to get a sense of how your colors work together.

**Practice Exercise: Building a Layered Pendant Design**

- **Goal**: Design a small pendant with layered soutache cords around a focal cabochon.

- **Materials Needed**: Focal cabochon, soutache cords in two colors, matching thread, beads, needle, and scissors.
- **Steps**:
1. Place your cabochon on paper and sketch a rough outline.
2. Plan two or three layers of cords around the cabochon, experimenting with different placements for color and bead accents.
3. Visualize where each layer will sit, adding small lines or circles to represent stitch points and accent beads.
4. Once you're satisfied, translate this design to your materials and start building the pendant.

## Staying Inspired and Experimenting

- **Finding Inspiration**

  Look to nature, fashion, or art for inspiration in colors, shapes, and patterns. Flowers, leaves, waves, and geometric shapes can all be translated into soutache designs. Use mood boards, color swatches, or photos to inspire your work.

- **Experimenting with New Designs**

  as you gain confidence, challenge yourself to combine techniques and try new shapes or color combinations. Don't be afraid to experiment with asymmetrical designs or unconventional color pairings they can lead to unexpected and exciting results.

# Chapter Four

## Crafting Your First Projects

This chapter will guide you through a series of beginner-friendly projects designed to help you apply the skills you've learned so far. Each project is crafted to build your confidence and allow you to explore different techniques, shapes, and design elements in soutache jewelry. By completing these projects, you'll gain experience in assembling pieces, securing layers, and incorporating beads, giving you a solid foundation to expand your creativity.

### Project 1: Simple Loop Earrings

1. **Description**

   these elegant loop earrings are a

great introduction to creating simple, balanced designs with soutache cords and beads. This project will focus on basic layering, adding accent beads, and finishing techniques.

2. **Materials Needed**

- Two colors of soutache cord (about 10 inches each)
- Small beads for accents
- Earring hooks
- Thread, needle, scissors, and glue

3. **Instructions**

1. **Prepare the Cords**: Start by cutting two 5-inch lengths of each cord color. Seal the ends with a touch of glue to prevent fraying.

2. **Create the Loop**: Place the cords side by side, aligning

the ends, and begin sewing a simple loop at the top. Secure each stitch as you work around the loop.

3. **Add Accent Beads**: Thread a small bead on each side of the loop and stitch it in place. Continue adding beads evenly around the loop to add sparkle and balance.

4. **Attach the Hook**: Once the loop and beads are secure, attach an earring hook at the top of the loop. Reinforce with additional stitches as needed.

5. **Finish**: Secure the ends with a final knot and add a

small dot of glue to ensure stability.

## Project 2: Layered Pendant with Focal Bead

1. **Description**

   this pendant project introduces layering and working with a focal bead as the centerpiece. The design includes loops and additional layers to frame the focal bead, creating a balanced and eye-catching piece.

2. **Materials Needed**

- Focal bead (flat-back cabochon or crystal)
- Three colors of soutache cord (about 12 inches each)
- Small spacer beads
- Bail or jump ring (to attach a chain)
- Thread, needle, scissors, and glue

3. **Instructions**

1. **Attach the Focal Bead**: Start by placing the focal bead at the center of your design. Stitch around the edge of the bead, securing it to a layer of soutache cords.

2. **Add First Layer of Cords**: Position two cords of contrasting colors side by side around the bead. Stitch along the cords to secure them around the focal point, keeping your stitches tight and consistent.

3. **Build the Second Layer**: Add the third cord around the first layer, securing with stitches. Continue to build

loops or spirals if desired, giving the piece more dimension.

4. **Embellish with Spacer Beads**: Place small spacer beads along the edges of the cords to add texture and contrast.

5. **Attach the Bail**: To finish, attach a bail or jump ring at the top of the pendant, securing it with stitches and a dot of glue for added stability.

## Project 3: Statement Bracelet with Layered Cords

1. **Description**

this bracelet project will help you explore larger designs and more intricate layering. The bracelet features multiple layers of cords, decorative beads, and a clasp, resulting in a striking piece that can be worn on any occasion.

2. **Materials Needed**

- Three to four colors of soutache cord (20 inches each)
- Focal beads and accent beads
- Bracelet clasp
- Thread, needle, scissors, and glue

3. **Instructions**

    1. **Plan the Layout**: Before starting, sketch your bracelet layout. Decide where you'd like to place focal beads, accent beads, and cords.

    2. **Create the Base**: Cut and align your cords, creating a

straight base. Begin stitching along the base, adding focal beads at the center or sides as per your layout.

3. **Build Layers**: Work outward by adding layers of cords around the base, following the bracelet's curvature. Secure each layer with even stitches.

4. **Add Decorative Elements**: Place small accent beads or crystals along the outer layers of the cords to add detail and shine. Space these elements evenly to maintain symmetry.

5. **Attach the Clasp**: Secure a clasp at both ends of the bracelet. Reinforce it with additional stitching, then trim and seal the cord ends with glue for a clean finish.

## Project 4: Elegant Brooch with Beaded Edging

1. **Description**

This brooch project allows you to practice shaping and adding an elegant beaded edge. With its layered cords and beaded accents, this brooch makes a refined and sophisticated addition to any outfit.

2. **Materials Needed**

- Focal cabochon or flat-back crystal
- Three colors of soutache cord (15 inches each)

- Small accent beads for edging
- Brooch pin backing
- Thread, needle, scissors, and glue

3. **Instructions**

   1. **Attach the Cabochon**: Secure the focal cabochon at the center by stitching around its edges.

   2. **Layer the Cords**: Position the first layer of cords around the cabochon, securing it with even stitches. Build additional layers, creating loops or curved shapes for added interest.

   3. **Add the Beaded Edge**: Thread small accent beads along the outer edge of the last cord layer, spacing

them evenly to frame the brooch.

4. **Attach the Brooch Pin**: Stitch the brooch pin backing securely onto the back of the piece, reinforcing it with several stitches. Conceal the stitches and trim any excess thread.

5. **Finish and Polish**: Secure all loose ends, adding a small amount of glue to any exposed knots, then gently press the cords to ensure they lie flat.

## Tips for Completing Your First Projects

- **Take Your Time**

    each project builds on your skills, so take time to get comfortable with each step. Don't rush through the stitching or finishing, as careful attention will give your work a more professional appearance.

- **Inspect as You Go**

    regularly check your work to ensure stitches are even and cords are aligned. Making small adjustments as you go can prevent issues later and ensure a balanced final piece.

- **Experiment with Color and Texture**

    Feel free to experiment with color combinations and bead placements. Each project can be customized to your liking, so don't hesitate to try out variations in your designs.

# Chapter Five

# Troubleshooting and Finishing Techniques

In this chapter, you'll learn how to handle common challenges that arise while making soutache jewelry, along with advanced finishing techniques to give your work a polished, professional look. From fixing alignment issues to perfecting your knots and seals, mastering these techniques will help you elevate your pieces and maintain their durability.

## Common Troubleshooting Issues

1. **Uneven or Misaligned Cords**
- **Problem**: Misalignment or twisting of cords can make your design look uneven or sloppy.

- **Solution**: Regularly check alignment as you stitch, adjusting cords so they lie flat and evenly spaced. Use your fingers to gently press and flatten cords into place. If a section is severely misaligned, consider carefully undoing recent stitches and repositioning the cords before continuing.

2. **Loose or Gaping Stitches**

- **Problem**: Loose stitches can create gaps between cords or make the piece look unfinished.

- **Solution**: Use even tension with each stitch, pulling just enough to secure without puckering. If stitches become loose, try reinforcing with backstitching or adding a tiny dot of fabric glue between cords to close gaps. Practice keeping a consistent tension to prevent loosening.

3. **Puckering or Curling Cords**

- **Problem**: Tight stitching can cause cords to pucker or curl, distorting the design.

- **Solution**: Keep a light, even tension and avoid over-tightening stitches. For sections that already have puckering, gently massage or flatten the cords with your fingers, or add a small drop of glue to help them hold their shape.

4. **Fraying Cord Ends**

- **Problem**: Frayed cord ends make the piece look unpolished and can lead to unraveling.

- **Solution**: Seal cord ends with a small dot of fabric glue or briefly passes them near a lighter to melt the fibers. Use scissors to trim any frayed threads carefully. Regularly check ends throughout your project, as soutache cords can fray during handling.

## Securing Beads and Embellishments

- **Attaching Focal Beads Firmly**
  For focal beads ensure they're firmly attached with backstitching or extra securing stitches. To prevent movement, position cords snugly around the bead and stitch tightly, reinforcing with additional stitches as needed.

- **Adding Spacer Beads with Stability**
  To add spacer beads along the edges or within designs, make sure

each bead is individually secured by stitching through it twice or reinforcing with a backstitch. Use a double strand of thread for larger beads, as this adds extra stability.

- **Troubleshooting Loose Beads**
  If beads loosen over time, re-stitch them or secure with a tiny dab of glue at the base. For larger beads, add additional anchoring stitches on either side to prevent wobbling or movement.

## Perfecting Finishing Techniques

1. **Knotting and Securing Loose Threads**
- **Technique**: When finishing a section or completing a piece, tie a secure knot at the end of your thread, then trim it close to the

knot. Use a small amount of fabric glue to secure the knot and prevent unraveling.

- **Tucking and Concealing Knots**: Tuck knots between layers of cords or beads to keep them hidden. Trim thread ends flush with the knot, and then gently press the knot into a seam or layer for a neat finish.

2. **Trimming and Shaping the Final Piece**

- **Technique**: Once your piece is fully stitched, examine it closely for any stray threads or uneven cords. Use sharp scissors to trim loose ends carefully. To refine the shape, use your fingers to gently mold the piece, pressing cords flat and adjusting any slight distortions.

- **Smoothing Cord Edges**: If you notice fraying or rough edges, lightly seal cord ends with a dab of fabric glue or gently pass them near a flame (if the material allows) to prevent further fraying.

3. **Applying Edge Beads for a Polished Look**

   Adding edge beads along the outer layer can frame the piece, giving it a finished, professional appearance. Stitch small beads evenly along the edge, ensuring consistent spacing and securing each bead with tight stitches.

## Finishing with Glue for Durability

- **Using Glue to Reinforce Stitches and Cords**

   Apply a minimal amount of clear-drying fabric or jewelry glue to areas needing reinforcement. This includes ends of cords, knots, and edges where layers meet. Avoid using too much, as excess glue can harden and alter the appearance of your piece.

- **Sealing Delicate Sections**
  For delicate designs with multiple layers, apply a thin layer of glue on the underside to add stability. Be careful not to oversaturated, as glue should not seep through to the visible surface. This technique helps maintain the shape and ensures longevity.

- **Securing the Back with Fabric**
  To add an extra layer of durability, consider attaching a piece of felt or suede to the back of the piece. Cut

the fabric to match the design's shape, then glue it to the back, covering knots and thread ends. This gives the piece a neat, finished look and makes it more comfortable to wear.

### Attaching Findings and Closures

- **Securing Earring Hooks and Pendant Bails**
  When adding earring hooks or bails for pendants, reinforce the area with multiple stitches, as this is a common point of tension. Apply a small amount of glue to the stitched area for extra hold, ensuring that the attachment won't loosen over time.

- **Attaching Clasps to Bracelets and Necklaces**

For bracelets or necklaces, securely stitch the clasp to each end of the piece. Consider using a sturdy jump ring for added flexibility, then reinforce with multiple stitches. A dot of glue on the clasp's base can ensure a firm hold without affecting movement.

- **Using Jump Rings or Split Rings for Flexibility**
  when attaching pieces to findings, use jump rings or split rings for added flexibility. This allows your piece to move naturally, reducing stress on stitches and improving durability.

## Polishing and Final Touches

- **Smoothing and Shaping**
  once the piece is complete, gently

shape it with your hands to ensure all elements are aligned and the overall form is smooth. Adjust any loose cords or beads and press the layers together to ensure consistency.

- **Cleaning for a Professional Finish**

  For a professional touch, use a lint-free cloth to gently clean the surface of your piece, removing any stray threads or smudges. If you used glue, ensure it's fully dried and inspect the piece for any visible residue.

- **Final Inspection**

  Check each attachment point, bead, and stitch for stability. Make small adjustments as needed, and ensure every element is secure before wearing or gifting.

**Practice Exercise: Perfecting Finishing Techniques**

- **Goal**: Create a small practice piece, focusing on finishing techniques like knotting, trimming, and gluing.
- **Materials Needed**: Soutache cords, small beads, needle, thread, fabric glue, and scissors.
- **Steps**:
1. Cut a 6-inch length of soutache cord, creating a simple loop or spiral.
2. Practice knotting and securing each end, trimming excess thread and sealing with glue.
3. Add a small bead to the edge and secure it with a final knot.

4. Attach a jump ring or bail, then review your piece, making small adjustments for a polished finish.

# Chapter Six

## Taking Your Skills to the Next Level

Now that you've mastered the basics, it's time to push the boundaries of your soutache jewelry skills! This chapter will introduce advanced techniques, inspiring design ideas, and methods to create more complex, sophisticated pieces. You'll also learn how to personalize your work, incorporate unconventional materials, and find your unique style within the art of soutache.

### Exploring Advanced Techniques

1. **Multi-Layered Designs**

   Advanced projects often involve creating depth and dimension by layering cords and embellishments. Experiment with:

- **Building Height and Texture**: Layer additional rows of soutache cords around a focal bead or central design element, creating a 3D effect.
- **Adding Variations in Shape**: Try incorporating twists, loops, and other shapes into each layer. This will bring a sense of movement and complexity to your design.
- **Securing Multiple Layers**: Ensure each layer is carefully secured with stitches, adding stability as you build upward or outward.

2. **Incorporating Intricate Beading Patterns**

Add complexity by working beads into your design with more intricate patterns. Explore techniques like:

- **Beaded Borders**: Use seed beads to create delicate edges along each cord layer.

- **Weaving Beads into Cords**: Stitch beads directly into soutache cords to form a continuous, integrated look.

- **Combining Beads and Crystals**: Mix bead sizes, colors, and shapes to add contrast and texture, enhancing visual interest in your piece.

3. **Creating Openwork and Lace Effects**

   Openwork designs bring lightness and elegance, with visible gaps between cords. This technique is ideal for intricate, airy patterns.

- **Spacing Cords Strategically**: Space cords intentionally and maintain even tension to create open sections.

- **Using Beads to Connect Open Sections**: Add small beads between cord loops to bridge gaps and reinforce the design without closing the open spaces.
- **Perfecting Lace-like Patterns**: Sketch out lace-inspired motifs, such as floral or filigree patterns, to plan your openwork design.

## Personalizing Your Jewelry with Unique Materials

1. **Combining Textiles and Fabric** mixing different types of fabric can add depth and character.
- **Velvet or Suede Accents**: Attach small velvet or suede pieces beneath

focal beads or as backing to enhance texture and luxury.

- **Lace Embellishments**: Incorporate lace sections within your soutache design for a romantic, vintage-inspired look.
- **Silk Ribbon Highlights**: Weave silk ribbon alongside soutache cords to add softness and color variation.

2. **Incorporating Natural Elements**
   Bring organic beauty into your designs by including natural materials:

- **Semi-Precious Stones**: Use gemstones like turquoise, amethyst, or lapis lazuli for a sophisticated focal point.
- **Wood or Bone Beads**: Add earthy elements with wooden or bone

beads, creating an organic contrast with the smooth cords.

- **Pearls and Shell Accents**: Pearls and small shell pieces add an elegant, beach-inspired vibe to your work.

3. **Using Metal Components for Edgy Designs**

   mixing metal elements with your cords can add boldness and modernity.

- **Metal Chains**: Weave thin chains through your design to introduce shine and contrast.

- **Metal Beads or Studs**: Small metal beads or studs can add a striking, edgy effect.

- **Charms and Pendants**: Incorporate meaningful charms or

pendants to create statement pieces with a personal touch.

**Design Inspiration: Creating Unique and Sophisticated Pieces**

1. **Exploring Artistic Themes**
   Draw inspiration from art movements or nature to create themed collections. Some ideas include:

- **Art Deco Patterns**: Experiment with geometric shapes, bold colors, and structured symmetry for a 1920s-inspired look.
- **Floral and Botanical Motifs**: Use soft colors and delicate spirals to evoke the beauty of nature.
- **Modern Minimalism**: Keep designs simple and elegant, focusing on

clean lines, monochrome colors, and subtle details.

2. **Creating Statement Pieces**
   Design larger, eye-catching pieces like necklaces, brooches, and headpieces that become the focal point of an outfit. Focus on:

- **Layering and Balance**: For larger pieces, maintain harmony by balancing the proportions of beads, cords, and embellishments.

- **Using Bold Colors and Contrast**: Experiment with striking color combinations and high-contrast designs to make a statement.

- **Mixing Textures and Materials**: Combine smooth cords with rougher elements like leather or crystal, creating an intriguing play of textures.

## Developing Your Unique Style

1. **Experiment with Color Palettes**
   Discover your signature color combinations by experimenting with warm, cool, or monochromatic palettes.

- **Create Custom Color Blends**: Dye your cords to achieve a unique color, or combine pre-dyed cords to develop a distinctive palette.

- **Use Seasonal Color Trends**: Stay inspired by exploring seasonal color palettes that reflect the tones of the season.

2. **Find a Signature Technique**
   As you grow more confident, you may develop a preference for certain techniques, whether it's intricate beading, layered designs, or openwork.

- **Perfect Your Favorite Technique**: Focus on refining your preferred technique, using it as a signature in your designs.
- **Combine Techniques for Complexity**: Mix multiple techniques, such as layering, openwork, and intricate beading, for complex, signature pieces.
3. **Experimenting with Proportions** Create unique designs by playing with scale and proportions.
- **Miniature Designs**: Try crafting small, detailed pieces like delicate rings or earrings.
- **Oversized Elements**: Experiment with larger focal beads or exaggerated cord layers for a bolder, avant-garde look.

**Creating Your Own Patterns and Templates**

- **Drawing and Planning**
  before starting a complex design, sketch a blueprint of your piece, outlining the placement of cords, beads, and layers.

- **Developing Repeatable Patterns**
  Create templates for favorite designs that you can reproduce or modify. This makes it easy to craft cohesive collections with a unified aesthetic.

- **Incorporating Personal Symbols**
  Add meaningful symbols or motifs, like initials, zodiac signs, or cultural symbols, to create one-of-a-kind, personal pieces.

## Advanced Practice Exercise: Craft a Statement Pendant

- **Goal**: Create a pendant that showcases layering, intricate beading, and openwork.
- **Materials Needed**: Focal bead or gemstone, soutache cords in three complementary colors, small accent beads, silk ribbon, and a pendant bail.
- **Steps**:
1. **Attach the Focal Bead**: Start by securing a focal bead at the center.
2. **Layer the Cords**: Build layers around the bead, incorporating spirals and loops as you go.
3. **Add Openwork**: Leave intentional gaps between cord layers, reinforcing with beads to maintain stability.

4. **Incorporate Ribbon**: Weave silk ribbon through the outer layer of cords.

5. **Finish and Attach Bail**: Secure the bail at the top, adding glue as needed to reinforce the attachment.

# Conclusion:

## Celebrating Your Soutache Journey

Congratulations on completing your journey through the world of soutache jewelry! You've explored the fundamental techniques, tackled troubleshooting challenges, and embraced advanced methods to elevate your creations. By now, you should feel empowered to express your unique style, combine materials, and experiment with intricate designs.

Soutache jewelry is not just about the finished product; it's an art form that allows you to tell your story through colors, textures, and patterns. Each piece you create is a reflection of your creativity and passion, making it a truly personal endeavor.

As you continue to develop your skills, remember that the beauty of this craft lies in the journey itself. Embrace every mistake as a lesson, and celebrate every success, no matter how small. Connect with fellow artisans, share your work, and draw inspiration from their journeys as well. Consider joining online communities or local craft groups to share ideas and gain feedback.

## Caring for Your Creations

As you create beautiful soutache pieces, also take the time to learn how to care for them:

- **Storage**: Keep your jewelry in a soft pouch or box to prevent tangling and damage.
- **Cleaning**: Use a soft cloth to gently clean your pieces, avoiding harsh chemicals that may damage the threads or beads.
- **Repair**: Familiarize yourself with basic repair techniques so you can maintain the integrity of your creations over time.

**Continuing Your Craft**

Keep exploring new trends, techniques, and materials to keep your work fresh and exciting. Consider:

- **Taking Workshops**: Engage in advanced classes or workshops to learn from other artisans.

- **Incorporating New Materials**: Challenge yourself to incorporate unconventional elements, pushing your creativity further.
- **Documenting Your Progress**: Maintain a journal or portfolio of your designs, noting what techniques you've tried and what you want to explore next.

## Inspiring Others

Share your passion for soutache jewelry with friends, family, or online platforms. Consider teaching a class or hosting a workshop to inspire others to discover this beautiful craft. You can help others find their creative voice while deepening your understanding and appreciation of soutache.

## Final Thoughts

The journey of creating soutache jewelry is as fulfilling as the pieces you craft. Allow your imagination to guide you, experiment without fear, and enjoy the process of creation. Your artistry is a celebration of individuality, and every piece holds the potential to connect with others on a personal level.

Thank you for embarking on this soutache journey. May your passion for this craft continue to grow, and may you create stunning, unique pieces that reflect your artistic spirit. Happy crafting!

Made in the USA
Columbia, SC
02 July 2025

60249620R00046